Fatty Liver Diet

Guide And Recipes to Reverse and Prevent Fatty Liver, Lose Excess Weight and Live Healthier

May Norah

ISBN-13: 978-1722846633

ISBN-10: 1722846631

DEDICATION

To all fatty liver disease patients and as many who desired healthy living.

TABLE OF CONTENTS

Introduction

Liver is the second largest organ in human body and it plays a very important role, helping other many organs in the body to function properly, its processes everything we eat or drink and filter any damaging stuff from the blood. The liver function is to processed nutritional fat and blood fat, liver contain some little fat and it is very normal, little fat in the liver causes no inflammation, when there is so much accumulation of fat in the liver cell it fails to function appropriately, it become a disease called fatty liver and it is reversible at the early stage.

It is our responsibility to keep our liver clean and healthy always by consuming healthy foods that guaranties healthy living and also prevents accumulation of fat in our liver cell. Healthy liver enables you to function appropriately and also have a better chance to live longer.

Fatty liver is when there is too much accumulation of fat in the liver cell and it causes no inflammation at the early stage but when it fails to be addressed, it get worse and can cause inflammation.

Fatty liver disease is a common problem for the liver and it is a silent health crisis affecting a very large number of people in the whole world.

Causes of Fatty Liver Disease

There are two major types of fatty liver disease, they are: (a) Alcoholic fatty liver disease (b) non alcoholic fatty liver disease

(a) Alcoholic fatty liver disease: this is a result of too much alcoholic consumption. The liver metabolizes most of the alcohol we drink, so it can be removed from the body. But the process of metabolizing can engender damaging substances. These substances can cause injury in the liver, which will lead to inflammations and cause the body natural defenses to grow weaker making it difficult for liver to metabolize fats as a result

More consumption of alcohol leads to more damage in liver cell. Alcohol is a direct poison to the liver and it can be corrected by staying away from alcohol for some time and it will naturally subside on its own.

(b) Non alcoholic fatty liver disease

Non alcoholic fatty liver disease (NAFL) is an early stage of liver disease and it is reversible. Unfortunately, if the fatty liver fail to be address at early stage it might lead non- alcoholic steatohepatitis NASH , which is a more serious fatty liver disease. Nonalcoholic fatty liver disease is not related to too much consumption of alcohol. There are some causes of nonalcoholic fatty liver disease, and they are:

1. Excess calories and sugar consumptions overpower the liver and prevent it from working appropriately and it lead to fat accumulation in the liver cell.

2. Diseases can also cause fatty liver as it associate with obesity, hyperlipidemia,type II diabetes, celiac disease, heart disease, metabolic syndrome and soon.

3. Side effect of some Medications such as amiodarone injection (Nestorone), tamoxifen (Soltamox), amiodarone oral (Cordarone, Pacerone), and so many others can cause fatty liver disease

Symptoms of Fatty Liver disease
Majority of patients with fatty liver disease experience little or no inflammation at the early stage. So, the early stage symptoms include: fatigue, loss of appetite, too much sweating, malaise, Nausea,

discomfort, excess weight in the upper abdominal area and so many other symptoms.

Symptoms of liver disease may expand if fatty liver is not reversed at the early stage, it will progress to cirrhosis and lead to inflammation causing scarring in the liver cell. The symptoms at this stage include: Dark urine, poor memory or confusion, increased bruising, Itching skin, swelling in the lower abdominal area (ascites) and so many others. If you have all or any of these symptoms, then there is a need to see a doctor without delay for health examination.

Reversing Fatty Liver With Foods

The best ways of treating fatty liver disease, despite of type before it damages the liver, is with the life style of exercising and dieting. Treating fatty liver disease (too much fat in the liver) is like treating obesity of the body, exercising and dieting can help the reversal fast. Fatty liver disease diet includes:

1. Eating of high-fiber plants such as whole grains and legumes

3. Eat very little added sugar, salt, Tran's fat, saturated fat and refined carbohydrates, Foods that are high in carbohydrates digest easily and such foods are converted into blood sugar immediately after consumption. Sugar and refined flours constantly increase insulin levels and blood sugar and also cause the fat in the liver to increase.

 Limiting the consumption of starchy and sugary foods, will help in reduction of blood sugar level and also lower the insulin level in your body.

4. Fruits and vegetables are the most powerful liver healing foods, fruits and raw vegetables help in cleansing the liver enabling it to function effectively.

Eating plenty of fruits and vegetables such as broccoli, cauliflower, zucchini, collards, arugula, kale, Brussels sprouts and so on, they are good foods that help in cleansing and repairing of fatty liver disease. Always add garlic and onions in your diet as they contain sulfur, which is great detoxifier, and also try to prepare your own salad dressing by yourself using vinegar and olive oil, and use it in moderation

2. Stay away from alcohol: Too much of alcoholic consumption has been confirmed to be the second main cause of fatty liver disease. It damages the liver and cause inflammation to the liver cells. Either you totally stay away from alcohol or reduce your intake of alcohol.

Best foods to include in your diet for a healthy liver:

1. Tofu: Tofu is low in fat and high in protein, it helps in reduction of accumulation of fat in the liver.

2. Coffee: Drinking of coffee helps to lower the amount of abnormal liver enzymes at risk for liver diseases.

3. Oatmeal: Whole grain like oatmeal helps in maintain weight and it a good source of energy to our body,

4. Walnuts: walnuts are very high in omega-3 fatty acids and it help to improve fatty liver disease.

5. Greens: Greens, like Broccoli helps in preventing the accumulation of fat in the liver cell. Constant consumption of Brussels, Spinach, Kale and Sprouts also help in losing and controlling weight.

6. Avocado: Avocado is very rich in fiber according to research it contain chemical that can help to protect the liver from damaging. It also helps in controlling weight.

7. Olive oil: Olive oil is very high in omega-3 fatty acids, olive oil is a healthy oil, it's healthier for cooking than other oil like butter and margarine, according to research olive oil help in controlling weight and lower liver enzyme levels

8. Garlic: Garlic is an herb that add flavor to our food. Adding garlic powder to our foods may help in reducing body fat and weight in an individual with fatty liver disease according to study.

9. Fish: Fatty fish, like tuna, sardines, trout and salmon, are very high in omega-3 fatty acids. Omega-3 fatty acids help in reducing inflammation and also improve the fat level of the liver and keep it healthy.

10. Sunflower seeds: Sunflower seeds are very high in vitamin E; it's an antioxidant that may defend the liver from more damage.

Exercise: Apart from modifying your diet exercise is an effective way to reduce excess fat in the liver according to research engaging in endurance exercise or resistance training a number of times a week can considerably reduce the amount of fat pile up in the liver cell, despite of weight loss occur or not

Foods not to include in your diet, if you have fatty liver disease

Avoid or limit the consumption of these foods that contribute in gaining of weight and increasing of blood sugar level.

1. Added sugar: stay away from sugary foods like, cookies, candy, fruit juice, sodas and so on. Too much consumption of sugar lead to high blood sugar which increase the accumulation of fat in the liver.

2. Fried foods: this is very high in fat and calories.

3Alohol: Alcohol this is the main cause of fatty liver disease it also leads to other liver disease if you fail to stop drinking alcohol in excess.

Salt: consumption of too much salty food can make your body to store plenty of water. Limiting your intake of sodium to less than 1,500 milligrams for each day will be fine..

4. Red meat: avoid the consumption of red as are high in saturated fat. Replace beef with fatty fish and poultry foods.

5. Refined Carbohydrates: Do not eat pasta, rice, and white bread. White bread means that the flour is highly processed, it does not contain fiber like whole grains and it increases the blood sugar.

The U.S. Food and Drug Administration has not yet approve any drugs for fatty liver disease

Discipline yourself to follow a good lifestyle and healthy eating plans, avoiding highly processed foods and engaging in exercise and avoiding too much alcoholic consumption can help in reversing fatty liver disease.

Recipes that helps in reversing and preventing of fatty liver disease

Breakfast recipes

Honey Nut Granola

Preparation time: 10 minutes

Total time: 30 minutes

Servings: 20

Ingredients:

4 cups rolled oats

1 cup sliced almonds

1 cup chopped pecans

1 cup raw sunflower seeds

1/3 cup canola oil

1/2 cup honey

1 teaspoon vanilla extract

1 tablespoon ground cinnamon

Instructions:

1. Combine the oats, and sunflower kernels, and nuts together in a large size bowl and stir.

2. In another medium size bowl, combine together the honey, oil, cinnamon and vanilla, mix, and then add to the dry ingredients and mix very well to combine.

3. Heat oven to 300 degrees F, divide and spread mixture into two separate ungreased baking sheets, and then bake for about 10

minutes, remove from heat, stir and take it back to the oven and bake for more 10 minutes or until golden.

4. Remove from heat and allow to totally cool before serving. You can put the left over in an airtight container and store in the fridge. Enjoy!

Apple, Lemon And Ginger Iced Green Tea

Preparation time: 15 minutes

Total time: 50 minutes

Servings: 22

Ingredients:

4 cups of water

2 apples,(seeded and roughly chopped)

3 - 4 tablespoons of green tea leaves

1 lemon zest

1½ tablespoons of honey

½ lemon (peeled and juiced)

1 tablespoon of grated ginger

Instructions:

1. In a medium size pot, combine lemon juice, honey, ginger, lemon zest and apple together and bring to a boil. Turn down the heat, and simmer for about 2 minutes.

2. Cover it and then remove from heat; let it sit for about 15 minutes.

3. Add the green tea leaves in a large jug.

4. Strain the water through a fine mesh on the green tea leaves, pressing all the juices from the apple, let sit for a minute.

5. Strain out the tea leaves. And decorate with lemon slices or apple. Serve. Enjoy!

Peach Syrup Custom Ingredient
Preparation time: 5 minutes

Total time: 10

Servings: 2

Ingredients:

1 ½ cup of peach

1 cup of water

¾ of sugar

Cinnamon,

Fresh ginger,

Nutmeg,

Instructions:

1. In a medium size saucepan, add all the ingredients and bring to a boil.

2. Reduce the heat and let it simmer until the syrupy is evenly

3. How long you allow it to boil depend on what you want. If it stays longer, it will have a stew peach flavor and if it stays lesser, it will have fragile peach flavor.

4. Add cinnamon, fresh ginger, and nutmeg, Strain with a colander and let it cool off. Serve and enjoy!

Frappe walnut coffee
Preparation time: 5 minutes

Total time: 10 minutes

Servings: 4

Ingredients:

7 Walnuts

1 teaspoon of Instant coffee powder

2 teaspoon of chocolate chips

2 scoop of vanilla ice cream

1 cup of Milk

1 teaspoon of vanilla essence

3 teaspoon of Honey

Instructions:

1. Put the walnuts in a blender and blend until smooth.

2. Then add other ingredients, the chocolate chips, vanilla essence, milk, vanilla ice cream, honey and instant coffee powder together in the blender and blend until well smooth and creamy.

3. Top with chocolate sprinkles and fresh cream and then serve chill. Enjoy!

Cold Coffee with Ice Cream

Preparation time: 5 minutes

Total time: 10 minutes

Servings: 3

Ingredients:

2 tablespoons of chocolate syrup

1 teaspoon of sugar

1 cup of milk

4 tablespoons of vanilla ice cream

½ cup of Ice cubes

2 tablespoons of Chocó chips

1 teaspoon of coffee powder

Instructions:

1. Add the milk, coffee powder, 2 tablespoons of ice cream, sugar and ice cubes in a blender and blend until foamy.

2. Garnish the sides of the glass with the chocolate syrup and then keep the garnished glass in the fridge.

3. Allow the glass in the fridge for 5 to 10 minute, before removing it,

4. Serve chill, top with Chocó chips and vanilla ice cream. Enjoy!

Chocolate mocha

Preparation time: 5 minutes

Total time: 10 minutes

Servings: 3

Ingredients:

Two espresso shot (4 tablespoon)

2 tablespoons of chocolate sauce

¾ cup of steamed milk

1 teaspoon of sugar (optional)

Whipped cream for garnish

Instructions:

1. Combine chocolate sauce with 2 tablespoons of hot water and stir to get a smooth paste, and then prepare the espresso into the cup.

2. Add milk in the steaming jug and then heat the milk with a steam stick.

4. Add the steamed milk to the espresso and garnish with whipped cream. Enjoy!

Regular Coffee with Cocoa and Milk

Preparation time: 5 minutes

Total time: 10 minutes

Servings: 3

Ingredients:

½ cup of strong black coffee

2 tablespoons of chocolate sauce or a tablespoon of cocoa

½ cup of hot milk

Whipped cream for decoration

Instructions:

1. Mix tablespoons of chocolate sauce or cocoa with 2 tablespoons of hot water and stir to obtain a smooth paste. Prepare the coffee and heat the milk.

2. Mix the coffee, cocoa, and hot milk together and then stir well.

3. Decorate with whipped cream and serve. Enjoy!

Homemade Peppermint Mocha

Preparation time: 5 minutes

Total time: 10 minutes

Servings: 3

Ingredients:

½ cup of freshly prepared brewed coffee

3 tablespoons of chocolate chips

½ cup of milk

2 tablespoons of crushed peppermint or 1/8 teaspoon of peppermint extract

Whipped cream candy

Instructions:

1. Brew the coffee, pour it in a mug.

2. Add peppermint (either the crushed or peppermint extract) and chocolate chips, and then stir until both the peppermint and chocolate are well dissolved, add milk and stir to mix well.

3. Garnish with crushed peppermint and whipped cream and then serve. Enjoy!

Simple & scrumptious Pumpkin Sunflower Trail Mix
Preparation time: 5 minutes

Total time: 5 minutes

 Servings: 1

Ingredients:

3 Tablespoon of natural pumpkin seeds

2 Tablespoon of natural sunflower seeds

3 Tablespoon of halved pecans

3 Tablespoon of dried cranberries (unsweetened)

Instructions:

1. In a medium size bowl, combine all the ingredients together and mix until well mixed. Serve. Enjoy!

Chocolate-walnut banana bread
Preparation time: 25 minutes

Total time: 1 hour 40 minutes

Servings: 12 slices

Ingredients:

3 large ripe and firm bananas

1 cup all-purpose flour

½ cup of semi-sweet chocolate chips

1 cup whole-wheat flour

1 teaspoon of baking soda

½ cup unsalted butter, at room temperature

¾ cup packed brown sugar

2 eggs

2 teaspoon of vanilla

½ cup of chopped walnuts

½ teaspoon of salt

Optional Ingredients:

2 tablespoons of ground flax seeds,

2 tablespoons of dark rum

Instructions:

1. in a large measuring cup or medium size bowl, Mash the bananas, it should be 1½ cup.

2. In a medium size bowl, combine the fl ours with ground fl ax seeds, baking soda and salt and mix.

3. In another large size bowl beat the sugar and butter until well combined, and then add egg, vanilla and rum, mix in the banana pureed.

Mango, Raspberry and Cashew Cream Parfaits
Preparation time: 5 minutes

Total time: 10 minutes

Serving: 4

Ingredients:

3/4 cup coconut water or drinkable water

1 ¼ cup of dried mango (slices)

1 ¼cup of cashews

1 cup of chopped fresh mango

1 cup of fresh raspberries

2 tablespoons of honey

¼ cup of toasted slivered almonds

1 tablespoon grated lemon zest (plus more for garnish)

A pinch of sea salt,

Instructions:

1. In a medium size bowl filled with warm water, put the dried slices of mango and let it stand until soften for about 2 hours. In another medium size bowl, repeat the process with the cashews

2. Drain out the water from the mango and put in the bowl of food processor and process until very smooth.

3. Drain out the water from the cashew and put the cashew in a blender, add the coconut water or drinkable water, lemon zest, honey, and a pinch of salt to taste, blend until very smooth.

4. Arrange in a parfait glasses, the cashew cream, layer fresh mango, mango purée and raspberries and then top with more zest and almonds, to your taste. Serve Enjoy!

Apple Carrot Ginger Muffins
Preparation time: 33 minutes

Total time: 20

 Servings: 12

Ingredients:

2 cups of all purpose flour

2 medium sizes of carrots (shredded)

2 medium size of apples (cored and shredded)

1 cup of buttermilk

1 teaspoon ground cinnamon

½ cup olive oil

3 eggs

1 cup of brown sugar

2 teaspoons of baking powder

1 teaspoon of baking soda

2 teaspoons freshly grated ginger

½ teaspoon ground nutmeg

¼ teaspoon ground cloves

½ teaspoon salt

Instructions:

1. Heat oven to 350F and set up a 12-cup muffin tin with paper liners.

2. In a large size bowl, combine together the grated carrots, buttermilk, brown sugar, olive oil, grated apples, and eggs, whisk until well combined.

3. In the same bowl, add the flour, baking powder, nutmeg, ginger, baking soda, cloves, cinnamon, and salt to taste, mix thoroughly with a wooden spoon until the flour are well mixed.

4. Pour the mixture evenly in the set up muffin cups; let it be at least 2/3 full and bake at 350f until golden brown for about 17 to18 minutes.

5. Store in a tight container, put in fridge for up to 5 or more days. Enjoy!

Salmon and Egg Breakfast Wrap
Preparation time: 5 minutes

Total time: 10

Servings: 1

Ingredients:

2 large eggs beaten

2 tablespoon of fat free Greek yogurt

1 tablespoon of fresh dill (chopped)

1 teaspoon of olive oil

A little grated zest and a squeeze of lemon juice

A handful of spinach, watercress, and rocket leaf salad

40g smoked salmon (slice into strips)

A pinch of salt

Freshly ground black pepper

Instructions:

1. Combine the herb, eggs. Salt and pepper in a pitcher and beat.

2. Preheat a skillet or sauce pan and then add the olive oil, add the egg and sauté until heat through or for about 1 minute, turn the egg to the other side and sauté until the bottom of the skillet is golden for more 1 minute.

3. Combine the lemon zest, juice, and black pepper and mix, and then scatter the smoked salmon on the egg wrap.

4. Drizzle on the yogurt mix and top with the veggies and then roll the egg wrap in pepper and serve. Enjoy!

Yogurt-Chia Pudding breakfast

Preparation time: 15 minutes

Total time: 12 hours

Servings: 4

Ingredients:

1½ tablespoon of chia seeds

2 cups of plain whole-milk yogurt

1 tablespoon of agave syrup, plus more

Sunflower seeds, and/or toasted coconut, Cocoa nibs, (for serving)

Instructions:

1. In large size bowl, mix together the agave syrup and chia seeds.

2. Cover and refrigerate for about 12 hours.

3. Top with sunflower seeds, or toasted coconut and cocoa nibs, you can sprinkle with more agave, if you want.

Chili Ginger Salmon

Preparation time: 20 minutes

Total time: 20 minutes

Servings: 1

Ingredients:

Fresh or preserved ginger

Salmon

½ of an orange or a lime

Soy sauce

2 Cloves of garlic (Chopped)

Fresh chili

Instructions:

1. Make the marinade. Chop the garlic, chili, and ginger into glide, and mix it together into a medium sized bowl.

2. Squeeze out the juice from the orange into the bowl together with the soy sauce. The quantity of soy sauce is completely depends on what you want.

3. Put the salmon in the marinade and make sure it is properly covered with the ginger, chili and garlic.

4. Then let the salmon sit in this marinade for 20 minutes or more.

5. Line an oven tray, with a foil and put all of the ingredients on the tray and then cook until tender or as desired.

6. Serve the salmon with greens, and potatoes or as desired. Enjoy!

Flaxseed milk walnut milk

Preparation time: 5 minutes

Total time: 10

Servings: 6

Ingredients:

¼ cup of flaxseed

6 cups of water

5 medjool dates (remove the stone and pitted)

1 teaspoon of pure vanilla extract

Instructions:

1. Pour 3 cups of the water in a blender with the seed and puree.

2. Strain with a strainer or a net to get the milk.

3. Add medjool dates to the milk and blend again.

4. Add vanilla to the milk and mix well to combine.

5. Best serve chilled. Enjoy

Lunch recipes

Beet and Nectarine Salad Recipe

Preparation time: 5minutes

Total time: 10 minutes

Serving: 8

Ingredients:

2 medium size nectarines (sliced)

2 packages (5 ounces each) spring mix salad greens

1 can (14-1/2 ounces) sliced beets, drained

½ cup of balsamic vinaigrette

½ cup crumbled feta cheese

Instructions:

1. In a medium size bowl, toss the nectarines with vinaigrette and the greens to coat.

2. Top with cheese and beets and then serve immediately. Enjoy!

Cashew-Curry Chicken Salad

Preparation time: 5minutes

Total time: 20 minutes

Serving: 6

Ingredients:

4 teaspoons of lemon juice

2/3 cup of honey Greek yogurt

4 teaspoons of honey

4 celery ribs (chopped)

1 teaspoon of curry powder

¼ teaspoon of garlic powder

3 cups of cubed cooked chicken breast

2 medium sizes of carrots (chopped)

2/3 cup of golden raisins

½ cup of cashews (chopped)

1/8 teaspoon ground ginger

¼ teaspoon salt

¼ teaspoon of pepper

Instructions:

1. Combine the entire ingredient together in a large size bowl and toss to coat.

2. Serve immediately. You can as well store the left over in the fridge for later use. Enjoy!

Tofu Summer Rolls
Preparation time: 5 minutes

Total time: 30 minutes

Yield Servings: 2

Ingredients:

½ (1 ¾) package extra-firm tofu, (cut into ½ inch planks)

1 tablespoon of soy sauce

1 tablespoon of vegetable oil

Kosher salt

1 teaspoon of toasted sesame oil

1 small head of lettuce (such as Little Gem or romaine hearts)

1 small carrot, julienned

¼ English hothouse cucumbers (halved lengthwise, seeded, sliced into half moons)

For serving use mint leaves, sweet chili sauce and lime wedges,

Instructions:

1. Heat oven to 350°. Put tofu on top of a paper towel-lined rimmed baking sheet. Place another layers of paper towels on tofu like 2 more and put a weighty skillet on top of it.

2. Let it drain for about15 minutes. Then remove the paper towels and slice tofu into ½" batons. 3. Toss tofu with vegetable oil and soy sauce on baking sheet; add salt to taste. Roast tofu, tossing once for about 20–25 minutes or when it starts to turn golden brown.

4. Sprinkle with sesame oil and toss to coat.

5. Serve tofu with lettuce, lime wedges, carrots, cucumbers, chili sauce and mint. Put it together before eating.

Note: you can roast Tofu for 2 days in advance. All you need to do is to cover it well and put in a fridge.

Baja Fish Tacos

Preparation time: 20 minutes

Total time: 20 minutes

Yield Servings: 4

Ingredients:

½ lb. tilapia fillets

3 Tablespoons of fresh lime juice (divided)

1 Tablespoons of Taco Seasoning Mix

1/3 cup of Mayonnaise

½ cup of Cheese

3 Tablespoons of chopped fresh cilantro (divided)

3 cups of coleslaw blend (cabbage slaw mix)

8 corn tortillas (6 inch), warmed

Instructions:

1. Evenly Brush fish with a tablespoon of lime juice; sprinkle the taco seasoning mix on the fish.

2. Spray cooking spray on a skillet and cook on a medium heat on both sides for 3 to 3 ½ minutes or until fish flakes easily with fork,

3. Drizzling fish with the remaining 1 Tablespoon of lime juice at the last minute.

4. Flake the fish into a small size with a fork.

5. Mix together the remaining lime juice, mix mayo, a tablespoon of cilantro and coleslaw blend

6. Top coleslaw blend with tortillas, fish, cheese and the remaining cilantro, and then serve. Enjoy!

Roasted maple beet salad
Preparation time: 15 minutes

Total time: 45 minutes

 Servings: 1

Ingredients:

2 tablespoons of maple syrup

16 small red and/or gold beets

1 tablespoon of olive oil

½ cup shelled walnuts

½ cup black olives

340g of baby spinach

1 teaspoon of salt

FOR DRESSING:

1/3 cup walnut oil

2 tablespoons of lemon juice

1/3 cup live cultured yogurt

3 tablespoons of orange juice

Salt to taste

Instructions:

1. Start by cutting off 1/2 inch of the stem from the top of the beet and then wash very well, but leave the skin on to protect the flavor.

2. Use little olive oil and maple syrup to coat the beet and put mixture in a low baking pan and place in oven at 350 degrees.

3. Roast for about 45 minutes while stirring every 15 minutes to coat.

4. Insert a tip of a sharp knife in the beet to check if they are ready, if the beet is a little crunchy in the meddle, Remove it from the heat and Peel off the skin,(but if they were organically grown, leave the skin on for utmost nutrition).divide each beet into four parts and set aside.

5. Make the dressing by whisking together all the ingredients the walnut oil, orange and yogurt juice until well mixed. Gradually whisk in the lemon juice, seasoning with a pinch of salt, taste and adjust taste if there is a need.

6. Divide the baby spinach 6 separate salad plates and heap a serving of beets in the middle of each plate and spread the walnuts and garlic stuffed olives on top.

7. Whisk and sprinkle 2 tablespoons of the dressing over each salad

Spicy Mango &Avocado Salad
Preparation time: 5 minutes

Total time: 5 minutes

 Servings: 4

Ingredients:

2 avocado (peeled and chopped)

2 mangos (peeled and chopped)

1 tablespoon unsalted and roasted sunflower kernels

1 large green onion (thinly chopped)

1 fresh Red Chile pepper (chopped)

1 tablespoon of olive oil

Salt to taste

Instructions:

1. Toss the avocados, mangos, sunflower kernels, onion, and peppers in a large size bowl.

2. Coat with olive oil and add salt to taste, served immediately, Enjoy!

Note: keep the remaining in an airtight container in the fridge for a late evening snack or next day lunch

Mushroom, tomato and avocado salad
Preparation time: 15 minutes

Total time: 30 minutes

Servings: 6

Ingredients:

2 Large firm ripe avocados (Peel and dice)

300g of mushrooms (sliced)

500g of cherry tomatoes (halved)

2 Lebanese cucumbers (finely sliced)

¼ cup virgin olive oil

1/2 Small lemon (juiced)

2 tablespoons of Mirin

1teaspoon of Dijon Mustard

1 clove of garlic (crushed)

1teaspoon honey

Instructions:

1. To make the dressing, Combine all the ingredients for the dressing in a jar with a cover and shake thoroughly until well combined. Set aside.

2. In a large glass bowl, put the mushrooms and Pour more than halve of the dressing on the mushrooms, stir to coat very well. Cover and let it sit until the mushrooms absorb the dressing very well for about 30 minutes or more.

3. Add the tomatoes, avocados, cucumber and bail to the mushrooms, and then pour the remaining dressing on it and gently toss to mix well. Serve. Enjoy!

Note: If you add 750g cooked peeled prawns it well become a main meal

Detox Salad with Lemon Dressing
 Preparation time: 25 minutes

Total time: 25

Servings: 4- 6

Ingredients:

2 cups of red cabbage (thinly sliced)

1 cup of parsley (chopped)

2 cups of kale (thinly sliced)

2 cup of broccoli (chopped in ¼-inch pieces)

1 red pepper (diced)

2 avocados (peeled and diced)

1 cup of carrot (sliced in matchsticks)

1 cup of radish (sliced in matchsticks

1 cup of raw walnuts (chopped)

2 Tablespoon of sesame seeds

Freshly ground black pepper to taste

For the dressing

½ cup of lemon juice

½ cup of olive oil

1 Tablespoon of agave nectar

1 teaspoon of fresh ginger, peeled and minced

A pinch of cayenne

¼ teaspoon of salt

Instructions:

1. Combine all the dressing ingredients to a blender and process until well mixed and creamy.

2. Combine all the salad ingredients a large size bowl, the cabbage, parsley, kale, broccoli, avocados, carrot, radish walnuts, and red pepper and toss well.

3. Slowly fold in the avocado to the salad, or you can also decide to add the avocado just before serving the salad (which ever you choose, your choice)

4. Add the dressing to the salad and toss until well mixed, and then transfer to serving plate, top with black pepper and sesame seeds. Serve. Enjoy!

Black Bean with Smoked Turkey, and Edamame Salad
Preparation time: 15 minutes

Total time: 15 minutes

Serving: 4

Ingredients:

2 cups of cubed smoked turkey meat

1 can (1 ¾ -2 ½ cup) black beans (rinsed and drained)

1 can (1 ¾ -2 ½ cup) unsalted corn kernels

1 cup of shelled edamame (cooked with the package instructions and cooled)

1 medium size red bell pepper (chopped)

½ c finely chopped red onion

¼ cup of fresh cilantro (thinly chopped) (optional)

1 Tablespoon of minced garlic

1 teaspoon of McCormick unsalted Original Perfect Pinch

1 teaspoon of Dijon mustard

2 Tablespoons of olive oil

2 Tablespoons of cider vinegar

1 teaspoon of Dijon mustard

4 cup of field greens

Instructions:

1. In a medium size bowl, combine together the onion, beans, turkey, edamame, corn, cilantro (optional), Perfect Pinch, garlic and bell pepper, mix to combine.

2. In a small size bowl, combine oil, mustard and vinegar and whisk together until well mixed.

3. Pour dressing over the veggies and turkey, toss well to combined and then add salt and pepper to taste.

4. Divide into 4 serving plates and put lettuce on each one of them and then top with the veggies mixture and turkey. Serve. Enjoy!

Chinese Chicken Salad
Preparation time: 20 minutes

Total time: 28 minutes

Serving: 4

Ingredients:

12 square wonton wrappers

½ (about 3½ oz) package of enoki mushrooms

4 cup of torn romaine lettuce

1 teaspoon of olive oil

1 can of slice water chestnuts (drained)

2 cup of cooked chicken (chopped)

2 Tablespoons of rice vinegar

3 scallions, sliced into thin round

1 rib of celery (thinly chipped)

1 Tablespoon of peanut oil

1 Tablespoon of sesame seeds

1 teaspoon of mustard powder

1 Tablespoon of hoisin sauce

½ teaspoon of sriracha sauce (optional)

Instructions:

1. Cut the wonton wrappers in ½ inch flooring, put on a nonstick baking sheet and coat the flooring with a cooking spray and the bake in a heated oven until for about 5 minutes or until crunchy and lightly browned.

2. In a large size bowl, combine the chicken, lettuce, water chestnuts, scallions, celery and mushrooms, mix well to combine.

3. In another small size bowl, combine the peanut oil, vinegar, hoisin sauce, olive oil, mustard powder, sesame seeds, and sriracha sauce (optional).

4. Whisk mixture to combine and pour over the veggies and chicken, toss very well to blend and to with the crunchy wonton skins and then serve. Enjoy!

Smoked Salmon, Avocado, & Egg Salad

Preparation time: 5 minutes

Total time: 15 minutes

Servings: 2

Ingredients:

Smoked salmon (chopped)

5 normal size eggs

Handful of fresh rocket and spinach leaves

1 avocado (peeled, and sliced)

Handful of cherry tomatoes (cut in half)

½ of cucumber (chopped)

For the dressing:

1 teaspoon of wholegrain Dijon mustard

½ of lemon juice

2 tablespoons of capers

2 tablespoons of olive oil

Instructions:

1. Place the 5 eggs in a pot and add enough water to cover the eggs, let it boil for about 10 minutes.

2. Remove from heat and put in a bowl of coldwater, to cool off before peeling the shell. Cut the egg in half.

4. In a large size bowl, add the salad ingredients, fresh rocket and spinach leaves, cherry tomatoes, smoked salmon, cucumber and avocado and mix well and then add helved eggs in the bowl also.

5. In a small size bowl, add all the salad dressing ingredients, Lemon juice, Dijon mustard, capers, and olive oil. Mix until well mixed.

6. Serve immediately. Enjoy!

Apple -Fennel Salad with Walnuts and Maple Dijon Vinaigrette

Preparation time: 15 minutes

Total time: 15 minutes

Servings: 2

Ingredients:

1 large apple (cored and finely sliced)

½ cup candied walnuts

1 small fennel bulb (cored and properly cut into thin strips)

Several shavings Pecorino Romano cheese

For the Vinaigrette

1 tablespoon of maple syrup

2 tablespoons of virgin olive oil

2 ½ teaspoons of fresh lemon juice

1 tablespoon of minced fresh chives

1 teaspoon of Dijon mustard

Salt and freshly ground black pepper to taste

Instructions:

1. In a small size bowl, combine the lemon juice, maple syrup, Dijon mustard and chives, whisk together.

2. Gradually sprinkle the olive oil over the mixture and whisk until well mixed, add salt and pepper to taste, Set aside.

3. In a medium size bowl, add the fennel strips and apple slices and pour the vinaigrette on it, and then toss to coat.

4. Divide the salad into two serving plates and then top with shavings of Pecorino Romano cheese and walnuts Enjoy!

Salmon and egg salad
Preparation time: 15 minutes

Total time: 15 minutes

Servings: 2-4

Ingredients:

2 cans (3/4 each) boneless (skinless wild salmon, drained)

⅓ Cup of sweet onion, (thinly chopped)

3 large of hard-boiled eggs, peeled (chopped)

½ cup of seedless cucumber, (thinly chopped)

¼ cup of fresh dill, (chopped)

2 Tablespoons mayonnaise

⅓ Cup green onion, (chopped)

⅓ Cup of plain Greek yogurt

2 Tablespoons mayonnaise

1 medium lemon, zested

½ teaspoon of paprika

2-3 teaspoons of fresh lemon juice

Salt and pepper to taste

tabasco sauce, (optional)

Instructions

1. Combine all the ingredients together in a medium sized bow and toss to mix well, add salt and pepper to taste and tabasco sauce, if you want.

2. Store in an airtight container and refrigerate for a day, stir well before serving. You can also serve immediately after preparation. Enjoy!

Olive Oil Dip for Italian Bread
Preparation time: 10 minutes

Total time: 5 minutes

Servings: 4

Ingredients:

¼ cup of olive oil

2 tablespoons of balsamic vinegar

1 tablespoon of crushed dried oregano

2 tablespoons of Parmesan cheese

5 cloves of garlic

Fresh ground black pepper, to taste

Instructions:

1. In a medium size bowl, add olive oil and press the garlic cloves in 5 different spots on the bowl.

2. Sprinkle balsamic vinegar on the olive oil and garlic, Parmesan cheese, oregano, and Season with pepper to taste. Serve. Enjoy!

Sweet Corn and Black Bean Salad

Preparation time: 5 minutes

Total time: 10

Servings: 6

Ingredients:

½ medium red onions (thinly chopped)

2 cups of fresh or frozen and thawed corn kernels

2 tablespoons of seasoned rice vinegar

1 tablespoon of lime juice

1 tablespoon of olive oil

4 cups unsalted cooked black beans (rinsed and drained)

1 red bell pepper (chopped)

1/3 cup fresh cilantro leave (thinly chopped)

¼ teaspoon of sea salt

½ teaspoon of ground black pepper

Instructions:

1.Pour water to a medium pot and let it boil, add the corn and cook for a minute, drain the water and rinse in a cold water (don't do this if you are not using fresh corn)

2. Rinse the red onion with cold water to remove some of its acidic flavor and sharp and then drain well and keep aside.

3. Combine the lime juice, vinegar, olive oil, salt and pepper in a large sized bowl and whisk together until well mixed. for the dressing.

4. Add the corn, beans, bell pepper and onion, toss until well combined.

5. Put in an air tight container and refrigerate for 2 hours, add the cilantro and toss before serving. Enjoy!

Dinner recipes

Chicken Provencal

Preparation time: 10 minutes

Total time: 30 minutes

Serving: 4

Ingredients:

4- 5 pieces of chicken

1 onion (chopped)

Olive oil

2 large of garlic cloves minced

1/3 cup of nicoise olives or kalamata olives drained (pitted and cut in half)

1 tablespoon of capers drained

2 ½ cups of tomatoes (chopped)

1/3 cup of white wine

1/4 cup of fresh basil chopped into ribbons (chiffonade)

Sea salt to taste

Freshly ground pepper

Instructions:

1. Properly season the both sides of the chicken with salt and pepper.

2. Pour the olive oil in a skillet and heat over medium- high heat, once the skillet is hot enough reduce the heat to medium heat, and then put the chicken in the skillet and brown the both sides of the chicken. Remove the chicken from the skillet and set aside.

3. Reduce the heat to low heat and then add the onion to the skillet, fry for about 2 minute or more, add the garlic and fry for more 30 seconds.

4. Add the white wine and tomatoes, cook until softened for about 3 minutes or more, put the chicken back to the skillet, cover the skillet and cook until the chicken is ready for about 25 minutes or more. Remove the chicken from the skillet for a moment.

5. Add the capers, olive, and fresh basil and stir, add salt if there is a need, add the chicken back to the skillet.

6. Top the sauce over the chicken and then serve with French bread or rice. Enjoy!

Tofu Coconut Curry
Preparation time: 10 minutes

Total time: 40 minutes

Servings: 4

Ingredients:

2 bunches of green onions

¼ cup of soy sauce (divided)

1(about1 ¾ cup) can of coconut milk

½ teaspoon of brown sugar

1 teaspoon of crushed fresh ginger

1 ½teaspoons of curry powder

2 teaspoons of Chile paste

1 pound of firm tofu (cut in ¾ inch cubes)

4 roma (plum) tomatoes (chopped)

4 cups of bok Choy (chopped)

1 yellow bell pepper (finely sliced)

4 ounces fresh mushrooms (chopped)

¼ cup of fresh basil (chopped)

Salt to taste

Instructions:

1. Combine the 3 tablespoons of soy sauce, coconut milk, curry powder, brown sugar, Chile paste and ginger, together in a large skillet on a medium heat.

2. Add the tofu, yellow pepper, tomatoes, mushrooms, and the green onions into the skillet. Then Cover, and cook for 5 minutes, stir but not often.

3. Stir in the bok choy and basil, Season with the remaining soy sauce and salt to taste.

4. Cook until vegetables are softening but crunchy for more 5 minutes.

5. Garnish with the remaining green onion, and then serve. Enjoy!

Bubble Loaf Garlic

Preparation time May Norah: 35 minutes

Total time: 35 minutes

 Servings: 32

Ingredients:

2 packages of active dry yeast (¼ ounce each)

¼ cup of warm water

2 teaspoons of garlic powder

1 tablespoon of dried parsley flakes

2 cups of warm milk

1 tablespoon of shortening

6 ¼ (or little bit more) cups of flour

½ cup of butter, melted

2 tablespoons of sugar

2 teaspoons of salt

Instructions:

1. Melt the yeast with warm water in a large size bowl; add 2 cups of flour, sugar, shortening, milk, and salt, mix until very smooth.

2. Add the remaining flour to get soft dough, mix until smooth and stretchy for about 6-8 minutes.

3. Put dough in a greased bowl grease also the top. And then cover and keep in a warm place to rise until doubled for about an hour.

4. Hit the dough down. Place the dough on a lightly floured surface; and then divide the dough into four, divide each portion of the dough into 12 pieces.

5. Combine the butter, garlic powder and parsley in a small size bowl and mold each piece into a ball shape. Yield: 2 loaves.

6. Put the dough in a two grease 9x5-inches loaf pan. If there is any remaining butter mixtures pour it on top of the dough, then and cover and let rise until doubled, for about 30 minutes or more.

7. Heat oven to 375° and bake until golden brown for bout35-40 or more, let it cool for about 10 minutes. Remove from pans to a wire racks. Serve immediately. Enjoy!

Oatmeal with Coconut &Mango

Preparation time: 15 minutes

Total time: 15 minutes

Yield Servings: 1

Ingredients:

2 tablespoons of unsweetened flaked coconut

1 serving quick-cooking or old-fashioned rolled oats

1 tablespoon of brown sugar

2 tablespoons of cashews (chopped)

½ cup of mango (chopped)

Instructions:

1. Heat oven to 350° F. spread the coconut flake on a rimmed baking sheet and toast, flinging occasionally, for about 3 to 5 minutes or until golden.

2. Use the directions on the park of the oats to prepare the oats, add the brown sugar.

3. Top with the mangoes, coconut, and cashews, and then serve enjoy!

Sauté Tofu Lime-curry

Preparation time: 5 minutes

Total time: 30 minutes

Yield Servings: 1

Ingredients:

2 tablespoons of peanut oil

1 (2 cups) package extra-firm tofu (cut into bite-sized cubes)

1 tablespoon of minced fresh ginger root

1 pound of zucchini (chopped)

2 tablespoons of red curry paste

1 red bell pepper (chopped)

2 tablespoons of maple syrup

3 tablespoons of lime juice

3 tablespoons of soy sauce

1 (1 ¾ cup) can of coconut milk

½ cup of fresh basil (chopped)

Instructions:

1. Pour peanut oil in a large skillet and let it heat on a medium high heat.

2. Add the tofu and sauté until golden brown, remove and set aside

3. Stir the curry paste and ginger in the hot oil and stir for a few seconds until the curry paste is aromatic and the ginger start to turn golden.

4. Add the zucchini and bell pepper; cook and stir for about 1 minute or more. And then add the lime juice, maple syrup, soy sauce, tofu and coconut milk.

5. Let the coconut milk simmer, and cook a 2 minutes or more or until the vegetables are soften and the tofu is hot.

6. Stir in the chopped basil before serving. Enjoy!

Meatballs Garlic And Sauce
Preparation time: 40 minutes

Total time: 20 minutes

Servings: 6

Ingredients:

2 large sized eggs (beaten)

1 pound ground beef

½ cup of bread crumbs

¼ cup Romano cheese or grated Parmesan

2 cloves of garlic (minced)

2 tablespoons of minced fresh parsley

2 tablespoons olive oil

Sauce:

1 tablespoon olive oil

½ cup minced fresh parsley

2 - 3 cloves of garlic (minced)

2 cans (3 ½ cup each) crushed tomatoes in puree

1 tablespoon o f dried basil

2 - 3 cups of water (divided

1 can (1 cup) tomato sauce

¼ cup grated Parmesan or Romano cheese

1 can (3/4 cup) tomato paste

2 teaspoons sugar

¼ teaspoon of pepper

Extra grated cheese and minced parsley (optional)

Instructions:

1. Combine the six ingredients for the meatballs together in a large size bowl.

2. Add the beef and carefully mix together. Shape the mixture into 12 meatballs.

3. Pour olive oil in large size skillet and let it heat over medium heat, brown meatballs, and then drain. Set aside.

4. To prepare the sauce: heat olive oil over medium-high heat in a Dutch oven, add the garlic and cook, stir for a minute.

5. Add the tomato sauce and paste, parsley, puree tomatoes, 2 cups of water, basil, cheese, sugar and pepper and let it boil, reduce the heat to low heat and carefully add meatballs.

6. Cover and simmer for about 3 hours until aromatic, stir but not frequent, add extra water if necessary.

7. Add extra parsley and cheese, if desire, and then serve. Enjoy!

Chicken with walnut and red-pepper salsa

Preparation time: 15 minutes

Total time: 20

Servings: 4

Ingredients:

4 boneless, skinless, chicken breasts

Fresh parsley (chopped)

Olive oil

½ cup toasted walnuts (chopped,)

1 small garlic clove (thinly minced)

2 teaspoons of cider vinegar

1 cup chopped roasted red peppers

1 teaspoon of honey

Ground cumin

1/8 teaspoon of salt

1/8 teaspoon cayenne pepper

Instructions:

1. Heat the barbecue to medium heat and brush chicken breasts well with olive oil. Put the chicken on grill.

2. Cover and Barbecue for about 6 minutes, turn chicken and continue barbecuing for more 8 -10 minutes or until it feels springy when pressed. Remove and let sit for about 5 minutes.

3. In a medium bowl, combine the vinegar, walnuts, garlic, parsley, honey, cayenne, cumin, red peppers, and salt. Mix until well mixed.

4. Slice the chicken and top with salsa and then serve. Enjoy!

Thai Chili Basil Chicken
Preparation time: 10 minutes

Total time: 15

Servings: 2

Ingredients:

225g or 7oz chicken thigh fillet (boneless and skinless cut into bite size pieces)

1 Thai chili (deseeds and thinly chopped)

1 ½ tablespoon of olive oil

1 scallion or shallot stem (cut into 2 inches lengths.)

1 cup of Thai basil leaves (loosely packed)

2 large garlic cloves (thinly chopped)

2 tablespoons of water

2 teaspoon of oyster sauce

1 teaspoon of light soy sauce

1 teaspoon of dark soy sauce

1 teaspoon of sugar

Instructions:

1. In a small size bowl, place all the Sauce ingredients and mix together to combine.

2. In large skillet, heat oil on a high heat, add the chili and garlic and sauté for about 10 seconds.

3. Add white part of the scallions or shallots and chicken, sauté for about 4 minutes or until cooked.

4. Add the sauce and cook for more 1minute until there is no water and sauce become slightly thickened.

5. Remove from heat and toss through green part of shallots or scallions and then the Thai basil leaves and stir for1 minute or more.

6. Serve immediately with rice. Enjoy!

Gorgonzola-walnut toasts
Preparation time: 15 minutes

Total time: 15 minutes

Servings: 6

Ingredients:

18 slices of baguette

150 g gorgonzola

Olive oil (for brushing or spraying)

1 cup of walnut (halves)

Honey (for drizzling)

Instructions:

1. Heat oven to 350F and place the 18 slices of baguette over a baking sheet.

2. Evenly spray the sides of each slice with olive oil and spread a cup of walnut halves in 1 layer on another baking sheet.

3. Put the two sheets in the oven and bake for about 6 minute until nuts are toasted.

4. Remove the nuts to cool in a rack, toss bread slices over nut and continue baking for about 4 minute or more until the both sides is lightly golden.

5. Let it cool completely before serving, spread 150 g gorgonzola evenly over bread slices.

6. Top each slice with walnuts and sprinkle with honey.

4. Add the flour mixture and use a wooden spoon, to stir until well combined.

5. Gently fold in walnuts and chocolate chips, rub olive oil in the pan, top evenly in a lightly oil 9 x 5-in. loaf pan.

6. Heat oven to 350f and bake in the center of oven for about 50 – 65 minutes or until tester inserted in the center of a loaf out without a stain.

7. Remove pan from heat to a rack to cool off for about10 minutes. Carefully turn the loaf in a rack, keep bread in the fridge up to 2 months or in a room temperature up to 3 days.

Smoked Salmon And Broccoli Frittata

Preparation time: 5 minutes

Total time: 10

 Servings: 2

Ingredients:

100g tender stem broccoli (trimmed)

3 large eggs

1 teaspoon of olive oil

25g smoked salmon (chopped)

1 tablespoon of fresh dill (chopped)

Salt to taste

Freshly ground black pepper

Instructions:

1. Place the broccoli in a pot and add water, bring to a boil for about 3 minutes or until soften

2. Drain in a strainer and rinse with cold water, keep it to be cold, and then drain.

3. In a medium saucepan or skillet, heat olive oil, add seasoning to the egg and beat.

4. Add the broccoli and sauté for about 2 minutes and then add the egg and sauté for more 4 minutes

5. Disperse the dill and salmon on the frittata and cook over a hot grill for about 2 minutes or more.

6. Cut into wedge and serve with salad. Enjoy!

Ground Chicken Burger Recipe
Preparation time: 15 minutes

Total time: 12 minutes

Servings: 4

Ingredients:

1 pound ground chicken

1 egg (lightly beaten)

2 scallions (sliced thin)

1 cup of seasoned bread crumbs

4 sesame seed burger buns

4-6 slices cheese (your choice)

Salt and pepper to taste

Instructions:

1. Combine the ground chicken, bread crumbs, egg and sliced scallions, together in a large size bowl, add salt and pepper to taste and then mix very well.

2. Shape the mixture into 4 - 6 patties and let the patties be flattened, because they will slightly puff immediately they enter the heat.

3. Put the patties on a heated medium-hot grill and heat for about 4 - 5 minutes on each side, or until ready.

4. Top burger with cheese and close grill for 1 minute to dissolve.

5. Put the buns on the grill for about 30 seconds on each side to warm, and then Put one burger on each buns and top as you desired, and then serve. Enjoy!

Vegetarian Quinoa Black Bean Chili
Preparation time: 10minutes

Total time: 40 minutes

Yields: 10

Ingredients:

1 tablespoon of olive oil (or less)

1 yellow onion, chopped

2 cups of water

1 stalk of celery (diced)

1 medium size carrot(peeled and diced)

2 tablespoons chili powder

1 tablespoon of cumin powder

1 teaspoon dried oregano

4 cups (or two cans) of cooked beans (I used a mix of black and pinto)

3 ½ cup of diced tomatoes with their juice

3 cups cooked quinoa

1 jalapeno, diced (optional)

1 red bell pepper, chopped

Salt and pepper to taste

Optional toppings:

 Greek yogurt,

Cilantro,

Sour cream,

Green onions,

Cheese

Instructions:

1. In a large size pot, heat oil over medium- high heat, add the onion, celery, peppers and carrot and cook, stir but not frequent, add the spices and cook for more 2 minutes.

2. Then add other remaining ingredients, reduce the heat to medium heat and simmer for about 30 minutes or veggies are soften. Add more water if desired.

4. Top with your desired toppings. Serve. Enjoy!

Cauliflower Bisque with Brown Butter Croutons

Preparation time: 25 minutes

Total time: 40 minutes

Yield: 4

Ingredients:

2 cups of whole milk

2 ½ cups of vegetable stock

1 small head of cauliflower (about 1 pound), separated into florets

3/4 lb. Yukon gold potatoes (peeled and sliced)

1 small size onion (sliced)

3 cups of cubed ciabatta bread

3 tablespoons of unsalted butter

1/3 cup of heavy cream

1/3 cup of pomegranate seeds

Chives for serving (Chopped)

4 sprigs thyme

2 cloves of Garlic (crushed)

Kosher salt

Freshly ground black pepper

Instructions:

1. In a large size saucepan, Combine the potato, cauliflower, milk, onion, milk, garlic, thyme, salt and pepper and bring to a boil over a medium-high heat.

2. Reduce the heat to low, cover and simmer for about 18 to 20 minutes or until veggies are softened.

3. In a large size skillet, over medium heat, dissolve the butter, swirling occasionally for about 2-4 minutes or until golden brown.

4. Add the bread and cook, stirring frequently for about10-12 minutes, add salt and pepper to taste.

5. Throw away the thyme sprigs and blend in batches in a blender until very smooth, add cream, salt and pepper to taste and pulse to combine.

6. Top with the pomegranate seeds, croutons, and chives and serve. Enjoy!

Salad recipes

Quinoa Spinach Power Salad With Lemon Vinaigrette

Preparation time: 5 minutes

Total time: 10 minutes

Yield: 1

Ingredients:

½ cup of uncooked quinoa

½ cup of diced cucumbers

2 cups of spinach (thinly chopped)

1½ tablespoon of olive oil

1 tomato (diced)

1½tablespoon of lemon juice

¼ cup of raisins

¼ teaspoon of salt

¼ teaspoon of ground black pepper

Instructions:

1. Rinse the quinoa very well in a medium size bowl.

2. Pour 2 cups of water and salt in a medium size saucepan and bring to a boil, add the quinoa and let it boil until the quinoa is softened for about 10 minutes or more. Drain out the water out from the quinoa and allow it to cool.

3. Combine the tomatoes, cucumbers, spinach, and raisins in a large size bowl, add the quinoa.

4. Combine the olive oil, lemon juice, in a mall size bowl for the vinaigrette; add salt and pepper to taste, mix very well to combine.

5. Pour the vinaigrette into the salad, toss to coat. Add more salt and pepper if you desired.

6. Serve. Enjoy!

Fresh Broccoli Salad With Lemon
Preparation time: 5 minutes

Total time: 30 minutes

Serving: 12

Ingredients:

¼ cup of cider vinegar

½ cup of reduced-fat mayonnaise

¼ cup of lemon juice

2 tablespoons of prepared mustard

¾ cup of cream cheese (melted)

14 cups of small broccoli florets (about 2-1/4 pounds)

1 cup of raisins

16 bacon strips (cooked and crumbled)

1/3 cup of red onion (chopped)

1 ½ cup of fresh mushrooms (remove the stems and properly chopped)

Lemon wedges (optional)

¼ cup of sugar

1 teaspoon of garlic salt

1/8 teaspoon of pepper

Instructions:

1. Blend the cider vinegar, mayonnaise, lemon juice, mustard, garlic, cream cheese, sugar and pepper together in a blender until very smooth.

2. Combine the mushrooms, bacon, onion broccoli, and raisins together in a large size bowl and pour the dressing over the salad, toss to well coat.

3. Place in an airtight container and store in the fridge until serving. You can serve with lemon wedges (optional). Enjoy!

Cucumber, Tomato, Onion Salad

Preparation time: 5 minutes

Total time: 5 minutes

Servings: 4

Ingredients:

5 medium size tomatoes (lengthwise halved, seeded, and thinly sliced)

¼ red onion (peeled, lengthwise halved, and thinly sliced)

1 medium size of cucumber, (lengthwise halved and thinly sliced)

2 tablespoons of extra-virgin olive oil

2 splash red wine vinegar

Coarse salt and black pepper to taste

Instructions:

1. Dress the tomatoes, cucumber and onions, with red wine vinegar, olive oil, salt Coarse, and black pepper to taste.

2. Set aside and let it sit for about 20 minutes, toss and serve with snacks of your choice. Enjoy!

Cucumber Salad
Preparation time: 10 minutes

Total time: 3 hours 10 minutes

Servings: 6

Ingredients:

2 medium sizes of cucumbers (finely sliced)

2 tablespoons of sugar

1/3 white vinegar or 1/3 cup of cider

1/8 teaspoon of pepper

1/3 cup of water

½ teaspoon of salt

Chopped fresh dill weed or parsley (optional)

Ingredients:

1. Put the cucumbers in a small sized plastic bowl.

2. Combine all the other ingredients together in an air tight container, except the dill weed and then shake very well until well mixed.

3. Pour mixture on the cucumber, cover and put in the fridge for about 3 hours to get a better taste.

4. Drain the cucumbers, drizzle with dill weed and then cover and put in the fridge you can all serve immediately. Enjoy!

Couscous and Vegetable Salad

Preparation time: 15 minutes

Total time: 45 minutes

Yield: serving 6

Ingredients:

1½ cup of water

1 teaspoon of salt

1 Tablespoon of olive oil plus1 teaspoon

1 cup of whole wheat couscous

1 can (1 ½ cup) chickpeas, rinsed and drained (reserve 3 tablespoon of the liquid)

½ c frozen peas (melted)

1 medium-size carrot (coarsely shredded)

1 small-size tomato (chopped)

1 small red or yellow bell pepper (chopped)

2½ Tablespoons of currants

2½ Tablespoons of fresh chives (thinly chopped)

1½ Tablespoons of pistachios or pine nuts

1½ Tablespoons of lemon juice

¼ teaspoon of dried thyme

¼ teaspoon of dried oregano

Angostura bitters (optional)

Instructions:

1. In a medium size saucepan, over a high heat, pour water, add 1 teaspoon of olive oil and salt, and then bring to a boil. Add the couscous and stir.

2. Remove mixture from heat cover and let it sit until it absorbed the liquid, for about 5 minutes, and then use fork to fluff the mixture.

3. In a large size bowl, place the couscous and add chickpeas (set aside the liquid) tomato, peas, carrot, currants, chives, nuts and pepper and gently toss until well mixed.

4. In a small size bowl, combine the oregano, lemon juice, thyme, bitters (optional), 1 tablespoon of olive oil, and then add the liquid set aside from chickpea.

Whisk together until well mixed, pour dressing over the salad and toss to mix.

5. Place salad in an airtight container and store in the fridge for about 30 minutes to blend the flavor and then serve and enjoy!

Greek Salad

Preparation time: 20 minutes

Total time: 20

Servings: 6

Ingredients:

2 large tomatoes (sliced)

1 head romaine lettuce (rinsed, dried and sliced)

1 red of onion (finely sliced)

6 tablespoons of olive oil

1 lemon juice

1 green bell pepper (sliced)

1 (3/4 cup) can pitted black olives

1 cucumber (sliced)

1 cup crumbled feta cheese

1 teaspoon dried oregano

1 red bell pepper (sliced)

Ground black pepper to taste

Instructions:

1. Combine the Romaine, tomatoes, onion, bell peppers, cucumber, olives, and cheese, together in large sized bowl.

2. In another medium size bowl combine together the lemon juice, olive oil, oregano, and black pepper and whisk until well mixed. Pour the dressing on a salad, toss and serve immediately. Enjoy!

Mushroom &Avocado Salad
Preparation time: 10 minutes

Total time: 15 minutes

Servings: 8

Ingredients:

6 medium ripe avocados (sliced)

2 tablespoon of olive oil

10 bacon rashers (chopped)

1 kg of tomato sliced

½ cup white vinegar

375 g of mushrooms (sliced)

¼ cup red wine vinegar

2 teaspoon of white sugar

½ cup chives (chopped)

Instructions:

1. Pour olive oil in a pan, let it heat over a medium-high heat, put the bacon and fry until crispy. Set aside.

2. In a serving plate, properly arrange the tomato, avocado, and mushrooms, and then combine the remaining ingredients and mix very well.

3. Pour mixture on a serving plate, drizzle with bacon and serve. Enjoy!

Winter Detox Salad
Preparation time: 10 minutes

Total time: 10

 Servings: 6

Ingredients:

2 cups of quinoa (cooked)

2 cups of baby kale (chopped)

1 cup of pomegranate arils

¼ cup of parsley (chopped)

2 blood oranges (peeled and cut into ½ inch pieces)

DRESSING

1/8 cup of vinegar

1/3 cup of olive oil

1/3 cup of blood orange juice

1/8 teaspoon of salt and pepper

Ingredients:

1. Combine the pomegranate arils, quinoa, oranges, parsley and kale, together in a large size bowl and toss.

2. Combine the vinegar, orange juice, olive oil, salt and pepper to taste, in a small size jar and whisk very well until well mixed.

3. Pour dressing on the salad and toss to coat. Serve. Enjoy!

Soup recipes

Low Fat Creamy Mushroom Soup

Preparation time: 10 minutes

Total time: 23 minutes

Servings: 5

Ingredients:

4 cups of water

3 tablespoon of flour

4 teaspoon of Better than Bouillon Chicken (or 2 chicken bouillon cubes)

5 oz shiitake mushrooms (sliced)

1 celery stalk

1 cup baby bella (sliced)

1 tablespoon of olive oil (optional)

Instructions:

1. In a blender, put the flour and water, bend until very smooth

2. Pour mixture in a medium size pot and heat over a medium heat3. Add the mushrooms, celery, chicken bouillon and olive oil and let it boil.

4. Reduce the heat and cover, simmer for about 20 minutes or until vegetables are ready. Remove from heat and then add the celery and a cup of soup.

5. Put in a blender and blend until very smooth, then put it back to the pot and simmer for 3 minutes or more over a low heat and then serve. Enjoy!

Broccoli-Cheddar Macaroni Soup

Preparation time: 5 minutes

Total time: 25 minutes

Serving: 4

Ingredients:

Olive oil

½ cup of red onion (Chopped)

1 clove of garlic (minced)

2 cup of small broccoli florets

¼ cup of dry white wine

4 cups of low-sodium chicken broth

1 cup of small macaroni

1 ½ cup of Grated Cheddar

¼ cup of chopped parsley (plus more for garnish)

Kosher salt

Freshly ground black pepper

Instructions:

1. Heat 1 table spoon of olive oil large pot over a medium heat, add the garlic and fry for about 3 minutes, add the wine and onions.

2. Reduce the heat to low heat and simmer for about 5 minutes and then add the macaroni, broth, and 1 teaspoon of salt and ½ teaspoon of pepper to taste and cook until ready.

3. Add the Cheddar, broccoli, and parsley when you are ready to serve, cover and cook until broccoli is light green and soften and the cheese is dissolved for about 1 minute.

4. Decorate with parsley and then serve immediately. Enjoy!

Broccoli Cheddar Soup
Preparation time: 5 minutes

Total time: 30 minutes

Yield: 4

Ingredients:

¼ cup of flour

¼ cup of olive oil

1 onion (chopped)

2 cup of whole milk

2 cup of low-sodium chicken broth

1 large head broccoli (thinly chopped)

1 large carrot (cut into matchsticks)

Baguette (for serving)

2 stalks celery (thinly sliced)

3 cup of shredded Cheddar (plus more for garnish)

Kosher salt

Freshly ground black pepper

Instructions:

1. Pour olive oil in a large size pot and heat, when is heat enough, add the onion and sauté until tender for about 5 minutes.

2. Add the flour and cook for more 2 minutes, add the chicken broth, salt and pepper to taste

3. Add the carrots, broccoli, and celery, reduce heat and simmer for about 20 minutes or until veggies are softened.

4. Add the milk and let it simmer for more minutes and then stir in the cheddar. add more salt and pepper to taste top with more cheddar if desired.

5. Serve with baguette. Enjoy!

Butternut Squash and White Bean Soup
Preparation time: 20 minutes

Total time: 3 hours 20 minutes

Yield: 4

Ingredients:

1 teaspoon of ground coriander

1 small butternut squash

2 clove garlic

6 sprig fresh thyme

¼ cup dried apricots

½ cup of couscous

¼ cup roasted pistachios

1 scallion

1 piece fresh ginger

¼ cup of fresh flat-leaf parsley

1 cans cannellini beans

1 cans chickpeas

1 small onion

1 teaspoon of kosher salt

1/2 teaspoon of Pepper

Instructions:

1. Combine 2 cups of water, ginger, and coriander, in a 5-6 quart slow cooker and whisk, add1 teaspoon of salt and ½ teaspoon of pepper to taste.

2. Add the onion, thyme, squash, and garlic, cover and cook for about 5 hours on low or 3 hours on high or until the squash is softened.

3. In a medium size bowl, put the couscous, add 1 ¼ cups of hot tap water, cover and let it rest for about 15 minutes. (Do this just about 20 minutes before serving)

4. Fluff with a fork and fold in the apricots, scallion, pistachios, parsley, and ¼ teaspoon of salt and pepper to taste.

5. Place half of the cannellini beans in a medium size bowl and mash with a fork until roughly smooth.

6. Turn the cooker to high and stir in the mashed beans, and then add remaining beans and chickpeas, cook for about 3 minutes or until evenly heated.

7. Spoon the soup in a serving plate and top with the couscous mixture and serve. Enjoy!

Harvest Pumpkin Soup

Preparation time: 15 minutes

Total time: 45 minutes

Yield: 8 serving

Ingredients:

1 large potato

2 tablespoons of unsalted butter

1 large onion

4 ½ cups of chicken broth

½ cup of heavy cream

1 can pure pumpkin

¼ teaspoon of ground nutmeg

Salt to taste

Freshly ground pepper

Instructions:

1. Place the butter in a large size pot and melt over a medium heat.

2. Add onion and potato, cook and stir but not often, for about 8 minutes. Then add the chicken broth, cover and let it boil, reduce the heat to low simmer for about 10-12 minutes or until the potato is softened. Stir in the pumpkin.

3. Blend the mixture in batches with a blender or with immersion blender until very smooth; add the nutmeg, ½ teaspoon of salt and 1/8 teaspoon of pepper to taste.

4. Increase the heat to medium high, return the mixture to the pot and bring to a boil.

5. Cover the pot and reduce the heat to low heat, cook for about 10 minutes, and then stir in the cream and let it heat through, add salt and pepper to taste if necessary. Serve. Enjoy!

Sweet Pea and Avocado Soup
Preparation time: 35 minutes

Total time: 4 hours 35 minutes

Yield: 8 serving

Ingredients:

2 tablespoon of unsalted butter

4 cup of vegetable stock

1 large avocado" (chopped)

1 medium-size sweet onion (chopped)

1 (1 ¼ cup) package frozen sweet peas (plus more for garnish)

1/3 cup of fresh lemon juice

2 cups of packed baby spinach leaves

1/2 cup of fresh mint leaves (plus more for garnish)

Plain Greek yogurt (for garnish)

Kosher salt

Freshly ground black pepper

Instructions:

1. In a large size saucepan, place the butter and melt over medium heat, add the onion, cook for 4 -6 minutes until tender.

2. Add the stock and let it boil, add the peas and continue cooking for about 4-6 minutes.

3. Remove the mixture from heat and add the mint and spinach and then stir, let it cool down slightly. Add the lemon juice and avocado and stir.

4. Blend in batches with a blender for 2 minutes per each batch, or with immersion blender until very smooth. Add salt and pepper to taste.

5. Put soup in the fridge for 4 hours to be chilled or up to 2 days. Thin with water as wanted.

6. Garnish with peas, yogurt and mint and serve. Enjoy!

Vegetable and Ravioli Soup

Preparation time: 10 minutes

Total time: 25 minutes

Yield: serving 4

Ingredients:

3 medium carrots (cut in halved lengthwise and sliced)

1 tablespoon of olive oil

3 stalks celery (sliced)

1 teaspoon of fresh thyme (chopped)

2 ½ package small cheese ravioli

2 cups of vegetable broth

5 cups of spinach (roughly sliced)

1 small onion (diced)

3 tablespoons of grated parmesan cheese

8 slices whole-wheat baguette

Kosher salt

Freshly ground pepper to taste

Instructions:

1. In a large size pot, over medium-high heat, heat the olive oil and add the onion, celery, carrots, and thyme, cook and stir but often, until veggies start soften for about 4 minutes.

2. Increase the heat to high and add the 3 cups of water and broth and then cover and let it boil, add the ravioli.

3. Reduce the heat to low heat and simmer until the ravioli are softened. Add the escarole and stir until wilted, add salt and pepper to taste.

4. Spoon soup into serving plate and drizzle with cheese and serve soup with bread. Enjoy!

Garlic Tortellini Soup

Preparation time: 5 minutes

Total time: 20 minutes

Servings: 6

Ingredients:

1 package (9 ounces) refrigerated cheese tortellini

1 tablespoon butter

2 garlic cloves, minced

1 can (1 ¾ cup) diced tomatoes with green chilies, undrained

3 cans (1 ¾ cup each) reduced-sodium chicken broth or vegetable broth

1 package (1 ¼) frozen chopped spinach, thawed and squeezed dry

Instructions:

1. Place the butter in a large size saucepan and heat in a medium high heat, add the garlic and sauté for about a minute, or until soften.

2. Add the broth and let it boil. Add the tortellini, don't cover, cook for about 7-9 minutes or until soften, and then add the spinach and tomatoes, allow heating through and then serving. Enjoy!

Drinks recipes

Melon Belly Slimming Detox Water

Preparation time: 5 minutes

Total time: 10 minutes

Yield 4 Serving:

Ingredients:

2 Mint leaves shredded

3 Thin slices of orange

3 Thins slices of lemon

Some Water

3/4 of ice

Instructions:

1. Fill a glass of cup with ice, add the water, mint and fruit, stir very well.

2. Cover and put in the fridge to sit for some minutes to blend well

3. Serve chilled. Enjoy!

Skeletal Green Tea Detox Drink

Preparation time: 5 minutes

Total time: 10 minutes

Yield 4 Serving

Ingredients:

1/4 Ice water

3 Slices of lime

Chopped up mint

½ cup of green tea (cold)

Ice cube

Instructions:

1. Combine all the ingredients in a glass jar and put in the fridge for 5-6 hours for the ingredient to blend well.

Place all the ingredients in a clean glass jar and put it in the refrigerator overnight.

Serve with ice and enjoy.

Apple Carrot Ginger Juice
Preparation time: 5 minutes

Total time: 5

 Yield 2 Serving

Ingredients:

6 normal size carrots

4 apples

2 in (2.5 cm) piece of ginger

Instructions:

1. Properly wash all the ingredients well and place in a blender and blend until smooth or through juice extractor and serve immediately. Enjoy!

Cucumber-and-Mint "Fauxjito"

Preparation time: 0 minutes

Total time: 5

Yield 1 Serving

Ingredients:

4 tablespoon of fresh lime juice

6 thin slices of cucumber, plus 1 long, thin slice for garnish

½ ounce agave Ice

½ cup of cold club soda

6 large mint leaves, plus 1 sprig for garnish

Instructions:

1. Combine the cucumber, mint leaves, agave ice and lime juice in a jar and shake well to combine

2. Strain out the liquid in an ice-filled Collins glass and add the club soda, and then stir only once.

3. Garnish with the mint sprig and cucumber slice. Serve. Enjoy!

Cellulite And Fat Cutter Juice

Preparation time: 5 minutes

Total time: 10 minutes

Yield 3 Serving

Ingredients:

1 Lemon (juice extracted)

2 Limes (juice extracted)

5 Grape fruits (juice extracted)

1/4 Medium size of pineapple (juice extracted)

1 Tablespoon of ginger

Instructions:

1. Combine the grapefruits juice, lime juice, and lemon juice together in a glass cup, add the ginger and mix.

2. Add the pineapple juice at last and fill with ice and serve. Enjoy!

Refreshing Pineapple-Citrus Super Detox Green Smoothie

Preparation time: 5 minutes

Total time: 5

Yield 2 Serving

Ingredients:

1 cup of pineapple (cubed)

½ cucumbers, with peel

½ cup fresh Italian parsley

2 cup of kale (or dandelion greens)

1 frozen banana (peeled and sliced after being thawed slightly)

1 cup of almond milk

1 orange (peeled and deseeded)

Instructions:

1. In a blender, add the entire ingredient, first the liquid, fruits and the greens and blend on high until very smooth and creamy for about 30 seconds.

2. Serve immediately. Enjoy!

Homemade Almond Milk
Preparation time: 15 minutes

Total time: 12 hours 15 minutes

 Yield 2 Serving

Ingredients:

1 cup of raw almonds (soaked with water)

3 1/2 cups drinkable water

1 tablespoon of agave nectar, or more to taste

A pinch of sea salt

Instructions:

1. In a medium size bowl, put the almonds, cover with water and soak for 12 hours.

2. Drain out the water with colander and put the almonds and 3 cups of water in a blender, blend on low speed for about 10 seconds, turn off the blender and then blend on high for about 1 minute. Remove from blender.

3. You can use cheesecloth or Put a nut milk bag on a large size bowl and then gradually pour the almond milk mixture into the bag. Gently press the base of the bag to release the milk. Throw away the pulp.

4. Properly clean up the blender and pour the milk back to the blender; add agave nectar and salt and blend milk until very smooth. Serve. Enjoy!

Coconut and Banana, Cacao Smoothie With Hempseeds

Preparation time: 5 minutes

Total time: 10

Yield 2 Serving

Ingredients:

2 medium bananas (frozen)

2 tablespoons of hempseeds

4 ice cubes

2 tablespoons of cacao nibs

2/3 cup of purified water

¼ cup coconut milk, unsweetened

Coconut flakes for topping

1 teaspoon of maple syrup (optional)

Instructions:

1. Place all the ingredients in a blender on a high speed until very smooth and thick. Add water according to your choice of consistency.

2. Divide mixture among two glasses and top with more cacao nibs, coconut flakes, and hempseed

3. Serve and enjoy!

Super Green Cleansing Smoothie
Preparation time: 5 minutes

Total time: 5

Yield 2 Serving

Ingredients:

2 bananas

3 cups of natural Girl Super Greens

½ cup of water

3 tablespoons chia seeds

1 cup of pineapples (chopped)

4 ice cube

½ cup of almond milk

Instructions:

1. In a blender, combine all the ingredients and blend until very smooth, add the ice cube according to your choice of consistency. Serve and Enjoy!

Burning Cucumber for Belly Fat

Preparation time: 5 minutes

Total time: 10 minutes

Yield 3 Serving

Ingredients:

1 large size cucumber (sliced)

6 Cups of drinkable water

1 Tablespoon of grated ginger

1 Lemon (sliced)

1/3 Cup of mint leaves

Instructions:

1. In a jar, pour the water and add the other ingredients into the jar cover and refrigerate overnight, so that the ingredients will blend well.

2. Serve the drink next day. Enjoy!

Pineapple Faux-jito

Preparation time: 5 minutes

Total time: 10

Yield 2 Serving

Ingredients:

½ cup of diced pineapple

4 teaspoons of coarse sugar

½ cup of chilled limeade

½ cups of chilled club soda

Ice cubes (for serving)

Lime slices

6 fresh mint leaves, plus sprigs for garnish

Pineapple chunks

Instructions:

1. Divide the pineapple into two in a glass and then add sugar and mint leaves and mix until the well combined and aromatic.

2. Add the limeade, ice cubes, and club soda and quickly stir to mix well.

3. Garnish with the pineapple chunk, lime slice, and sprig of mint. Serve. Enjoy!

Peaches and Tea Punch
Preparation time: 5 minutes

Total time: 10

Yield 3 Serving

Ingredients:

¼ cup of vodka

2 tablespoon of peach schnapps

2 slices of lemon

Half of a fresh peach (sliced)

Lipton's iced tea (for topping)

Instructions:

1. In a large size jar, add the peach schnapps, vodka, iced tea, lemon slices, and the fresh peach, close the jar and give it a thorough shake to combine.

2. Put in the refrigerator until you are ready to serve. Enjoy!

Lemon, Apple, Berry, and Cider Vinegar Drink
Preparation time: 5 minutes

Total time: 20 minutes

Yield 2 Serving

Ingredients:

1 Tablespoon of apple cider vinegar

2 Tablespoons of fresh frozen berries

1 Tablespoon of lemon Juice

4 cups of Water

2 ice cube

½ teaspoon of honey (optional)

Instructions:

1. Put the berries in the base of a glass cup and add honey (optional) use the back of a spoon to mash the berries and honey together.

2. Add the lemon juice and apple cider vinegar to the cup and then add the ice and water

3. Mix very well to blend for about a minute and then serve. Enjoy!

Iced Green Tea With Lemon Apple, And Ginger

Preparation time: 5 minutes

Total time: 15

Yield 2 Serving

Ingredients:

4 cups of water

1½ tablespoons of honey

4 tablespoons tea leaves (or 4 green tea bags)

½ lemon juice

1 tablespoon of grated ginger

1 Zest lemon

2 apples, (seeded and coarsely chopped)

Instructions:

1. In a medium size pot, combine together the apple, lemon juice, ginger, honey, lemon zest, and water and bring to a boil, reduce the heat a little and simmer for about 2 minute.

2. Cover the pot and remove from heat, and let sit for about 15 minutes.

3. In a large jug add the green tea leaves. Sieve the water mixture from the pot through a net on the green tea leaves, press out all the juices from the apple, and then let it sit for about a minute.

4. Sieve the tea leaves and garnish with slices of lemon or apple. Serve. Enjoy!

Shamrock Shakes

Preparation time: 10 minutes

Total time: 10

Yield 2 Serving

Ingredients:

2 cups of vanilla ice cream

9 drops of green food coloring

1 ¼ cups of milk

¼ teaspoon mint extract

Optional ingredients:

2 tablespoons of whipped cream

2 tablespoons of chocolate syrup

½ teaspoon green decorator sugar

Instructions:

1. In a blender or food processor, combine the milk, ice cream, mint extract, and food coloring together and blend until very smooth.

2. Sprinkle the chocolate syrup inside of the 2 high glasses and shake very well.

3. Top with green decorator sugar and whipped cream (if you are using).serve. Enjoy!

Raspberry Sparkling Limeade

Preparation time: 10 minutes

Total time: 10

Yield 6 Serving

Ingredients:

2/3 cup freshly squeezed lime juice

½ cup granulated sugar

2 cups of fresh raspberries

4 cups of lime flavored sparkling water

Slices of lime,

Raspberries and mint for garnish (optional)

Instructions:

1. Combine the sugar and lime juice together in a jug, and stir until the sugar is melt completely. 2. Place a small sieve on top of the opening of the jug, and press the raspberries through the sieve with a spoon, do this in batches.

3. Throw the remaining raspberry seeds and pulp away.

4. Add the sparkling water to the jug and stir together. Add the raspberries, mint sprigs and lime slices to the jug.

5. Best serve immediately or put in the fridge to chill and serve the same day.(if you preferred) enjoy!

Mixed Berry Smoothie
Preparation time: 5 minutes

Total time: 10

Yield 2 Serving

Ingredients:

1 ½ cups of apple juice (or other flavor of your choice)

1 ½ cups of frozen mixed berries

1 sliced of banana

¾ cup of vanilla Greek yogurt

Optional garnish: fresh berries and mint sprigs

1 tablespoon of honey (optional)

Instructions:

1. In a blender, combine the banana, berries, apple juice, and yogurt and blend until very smooth, add little liquid if too thick about ¼ cup.

2. Taste and honey (optional) divide mixture in two glasses and decorate with mint and sprigs fresh berries (optional)

3. Serve and enjoy

Watermelon Juice
Preparation time: 5 minutes

Total time: 10 minutes

Yield 1 Serving

Ingredients:

2 cups of watermelon (seeded and chopped)

1/4 teaspoon of black pepper

1 cup of ice (crushed)

2 teaspoons of honey

Fresh mint (optional for garnishing)

Instructions:

1. In a blender, Combine watermelon, honey, ice, and black pepper and blend until very smooth

2. Garnish with mint if desired. Stir well before serving and Serve chilled. Enjoy!

Berry Fat Flusher Drink

Preparation time: 5minutes

Total time: 30 minutes

Yield 1 Serving

Ingredients:

4 Raspberries

4 Blueberries

8 Oz of water

4 Slices of cucumber

Ice

Instructions:

1.In a glass jar, pour the water and add all the other ingredients, put in a fridge for about 30 minute, this will enable the water to absorb the ingredients well.

2. Add the ice and serve. Enjoy!

Coconut Pineapple Smoothie
Preparation time: 5 minutes

Total time: 5

Yield 2 Serving

Ingredients:

1 cup of Almond Breeze Almond milk, Coconut milk, Blend or Original variety

1 fresh banana or frozen

¼ cup of sweetened coconut flaked

2 cups of frozen pineapple

Garnishes optional

2 coarse sugars sprigs of mint

2 pineapple wedges

2 lime wedges

Instructions:

1. In a blender, place the banana, coconut, almond milk, and pineapple and blend until very smooth.

2. You can serve immediately without garnishing, (you can as well garnish if you desire)

Queen Bee Cocktail Recipe
Preparation time: 10 minutes

Total time: 25 minutes

Yield 4 Serving

Ingredients:

2 tablespoons of Tia Maria

4 tablespoons of lime vodka

1 tablespoon of dry sherry

1. In a Shaker, combine all the ingredients together and shake very well, add ice cubes, and strain into a martini glass.

2. Allow the ice cubes to weaken the drink a bit, if desired.

3. Decorate with a lime wedge or a few coffee beans dropped into the drink.

Snacks recipes:

Raspberry Bombs

Preparation time: 5 minutes

Total time: 10

Servings: 24

Ingredients:

1 cup of raw almonds

1 cup frozen raspberries

½ cup of desiccated coconut

3 medjool dates (seeds removed)

1 teaspoon of coconut oil

Chocolate coating (optional)

40g dark chocolate (I use 70% cacao)

This amount will coat half of the balls - double the recipe to coat all

Instructions:

1. In a blender or food processor, place the almonds and process, add the remaining other ingredients and then keep processing.

2. Scrape down the sides of the food processor if necessary and continue processing until well combined.

3. Roll the mixture into balls and put in the freezer to sit.

This is optional,

4. Melt the chocolate, add the coconut oil and mix well.

5. Dip raspberry bombs into melted chocolate then put on the tray wrinkly with baking paper and pick the ball with tooth pick and dip it in the chocolate mixture and then store in the freezer to sit.

6. It stays longer when you store it in the freezer. Enjoy!

Scrumptious Tuna Sandwich
Preparation time: 10 minutes

Total time: 20 minutes

Servings: 6

Ingredients:

1 can of tune flakes in oil

Coriander and herb sauce

Mayo

Hot chili sauce

Bread

Lettuce

Instructions:

1. Drain out all the oil from the tuna can.

2. In a large size bowl, add either 1 teaspoon of herb sauce or mayo or coriander, add hot chili sauce and mix well.

3. Coat with the lettuce and tuna mix and serve with your bread. Enjoy!

Fish Kebabs / Fish Kebab Burgers

Preparation time: 10 minutes

Total time: 20 minutes

 Servings: 6

Ingredients:

1 tin of salmon or tuna

Olive Oil (for frying)

1 packet of mashed potato flakes

½teaspoon of paprika

1 teaspoon of mixed herbs

1 lemon Juice

1 egg

Bread crumbs

½ teaspoon of salt

A Pinch of pepper

Instructions:

1. To make a mash potato, put water in a pot and add the potato flakes, bring to a boil.

2. Drain the fish, flake with clean hands, add potato and mix very well.

4. Add other ingredients, paprika, mixed herbs, and lemon Juice

5) Shape into pies / kebabs (about 2cm in thick circles)

6) Heat the oil over a medium- high heat and dip pies into a beaten egg, and then breadcrumbs, low fry until golden brown on both side.

7. Put either burger buns or pitta bread with lettuce and ketchup for fish kebab burgers

Lemon Cookies
Preparation time: 15 minutes

Total time: 50 minutes

Servings: 22

Ingredients:

2¼ cups of flour

1 cup of butter, (softened)

1½ cups of sugar

1 normal size egg

1 teaspoon of lemon juice

1 Tablespoon of Lemon zest

1 teaspoon of vanilla

½ teaspoon of salt

½ teaspoon of baking powder

Lemon glaze

1½ cup of powdered sugar

1 Tablespoon of lemon juice

1 Tablespoon of lemon zest

1 Tablespoon of milk

¼ teaspoon of vanilla

Instructions:

1. Combine together, egg, butter, and sugar in a large size bowl and mix with any mixer of your choice (either hand mixer or electric mixer) mix until creamy.

2. Add lemon zest, vanilla, lemon juice, flour, baking powder and salt and then mix until well combined.

3. Roll the in 1 inch balls each and put in a greased cookie sheet, let the dough be 2 " apart from one another.

4. Make round shape with the dough about 1 inch balls and put on greased cookie sheet. Space the cookie dough balls 2 inches gape from each other.

5. Bake in batches at 350 degrees F until lightly golden on the edges of the cookies, at least for about 8-10 minutes.

6. Remove cookies from the heat to cool off on the baking sheet for about 2 minutes and then transfer to a wire rack to cool off totally.

7. In a medium sized bowl, combine together the glaze ingredients and whisk well until very smooth.

8. Sprinkle the glaze on the cookie as you desired and then let it cool off totally before serving. Enjoy!

Nut & Seed Banana Oat Snack Bars
Preparation time: 10 minutes

Total time: 40 minutes

Servings: 6

Ingredients:

1 cup of rolled oats

½ cup shelled sunflower seeds

¼ cup walnuts (roughly chopped)

½ cup of pepitas (shelled pumpkin seeds)

¼cup almonds (roughly chopped)

¼cup dried cherries or pitted dates, (chopped)

½teaspoon of cinnamon

3 small ripe bananas (about 1 ¼ cups after pureeing)

1 teaspoon of vanilla

Olive oil, for greasing pan

½teaspoon of salt

Instructions:

1. Heat oven to 350°F and oil the base of the pan and the sides of a 9-by-9-inch square pan

2. Put the bananas, cinnamon, vanilla, and salt in a blender or in the bowl of small food processor and process until smooth.

3. Combine the oats, nuts, seeds, and dried fruit. Place the bananas, vanilla, salt and cinnamon in a large size bowl.

4. Pour the banana puree on the oat mixture and stir until all the dry ingredients are equally moist. Press mixture evenly into the bottom of the pan.

5. Bake until firm and lightly browned on the edges for about 30 minutes, remove from the heat to cool off completely and then cut into 6 bars.

6. Wrap them separately and store them in the freezer container for 3 up to months or in an airtight container for some days. Enjoy!

Vanilla fruit snack balls

Preparation time: 5 minutes

Total time: 10

Servings: 24

Ingredients:

10 large Mejdool dates (stones removed)

1 cup of raw almonds

1 cup of toasted walnuts

½ cup Raisins

1 cup dried apple slices (the softer style)

6 Dried apricots

½ teaspoon of vanilla powder

1 serving of coconut threads, for rolling

Instructions:

1. In a small size bowl of warm water, place and cover the apple slices to soak and soften for about 10 minutes.

2. Place other remaining ingredients in a food processor, apart from coconut, also add the soaked and soften apple slices in the same food processor and process (don't let it be to smooth) leaving some particle in the nuts and fruit.

3. Roll balls into an evenly size and then roll in the coconut thread to coat.

4. Store in a tight container and keep in the freezer. Enjoy!

Healthy "Nutella" Bliss Balls
Preparation time: 5 minutes

Total time: 10

Servings: 14

Ingredients:

1 cup of hazelnuts

1 cup of pitted dates

2 tablespoons of cacao

1 tablespoon of pure maple syrup

1 tablespoon of Chocolate

Instructions:

1. In a food processor, combine all the ingredients and process, add a little of water if necessary.

2. Roll balls into an evenly size and then use 1 teaspoon of the choc mixture and roll into ball to coat.

The end

Printed in Great Britain
by Amazon